A Poetic Journey

Selene A. Olguin

A Poetic Journey

Published by Spines Publishing Platform

ISBN: 979-8-89569-751-1

A Poetic Journey

Selene A. Olguin

Illustrated By: Rose Olguin

LIFE II
VANITY
A NEW YEAR
ANIMALS
THESE OLD WALLS
AUTUMN
KINDNESS

Contents

Age 12

Animals!

While some are big and some are small, some have teeth and maybe claws. Cute and sweet, some may be like chinchillas, raccoons, and honeybees.

One may be your friend, like a dog, a cat, or a country rat. Maybe a friend has a pig or a frog, but any type of animal will be a ball.

Winter Storm!

As I sit in my home with my warm soup, a storm is brewing and blowing towards you.
The snow is so blue, and the trees so bare. Not a soul dare step foot out there.
I still sit inside with a hot chocolate by my side. Time had passed, and then you came inside.
Poured on with snow, drenched to the bone! You just finished shoveling the snow.

Summer Breeze

As I see the tall green tree with all the leaves through a summer breeze. I sit in the shade that it provides, putting myself in a world of silence. Slowly, the wind passes through my hair and the whistling noise in my ear, something I have not felt in a while; glad to feel it from time to time.

Forest

The birds sing sweetly in the trees, and the leaves sway gently in the breeze.

The tiniest animal burrows into a tunnel while a stream flows all so subtly.

The brave wolves run through the grass as a tiny rabbit tries to pass.

Even though some things move faster or slower than others, God created everything in order.

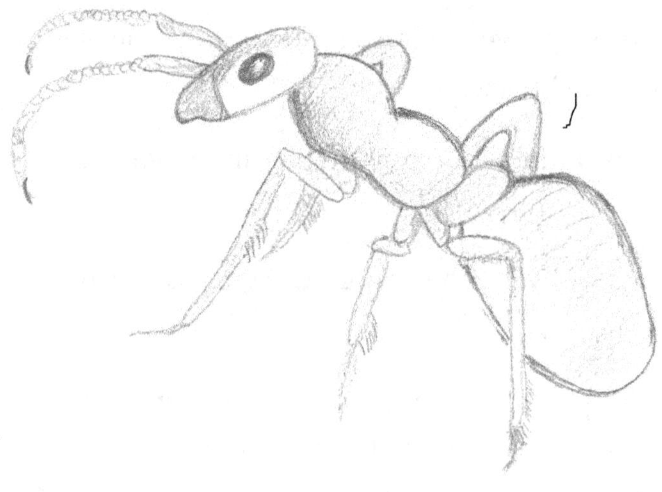

Minuscule

Tiny things are everywhere in the sky and in the summer air.

Dogs, for example, can be small, have short hair, and be not that tall.

Look at germs, you can't even see them, but they are there for a reason.

Insects are almost always tiny, like sugar ants and fleas, yet they all can do some wonderful things. So, if you feel that you're so small, just remember all the minuscules.

The Surprise in the Bag!

The first time we met, it was in a bag, and it did not sag. I set it down on my living room floor, and I heard it chirp, chirping galore. I gazed at the bag, wondering what it could be. So, I peeked my head in, and you won't believe what I could see! A tiny gray chick with a big fluffy tail and a little brown beak that went peep, peep, peep.

Sunshine

It clears a path and shows a way; it shines brightly every day. We go out, and we play; it will never go away. Just wake up and look outside; you will see that it gives hope to the inside. Remember to turn that frown upside down every day you feel let down.

Water

As it flows gently, softly down the stream, down a waterfall, or a creek.

Water holds memories and stories untold, calmly, it can be soothing, yet it can be strong and moving. It is used for many things like nourishment and health and it is very important for life itself.

Autumn

The colors change from red to gold as time passes by, from young to old. A new year starts with a beautiful death before a jump back to life full of wealth. The leaves slowly fall, and the cool winds blow; I hear the water flow in the creek down below. The calming smell of pumpkin spice and a pumpkin pie at a reasonable price. So many possibilities for the next coming year, time for me to spend time with my peers!

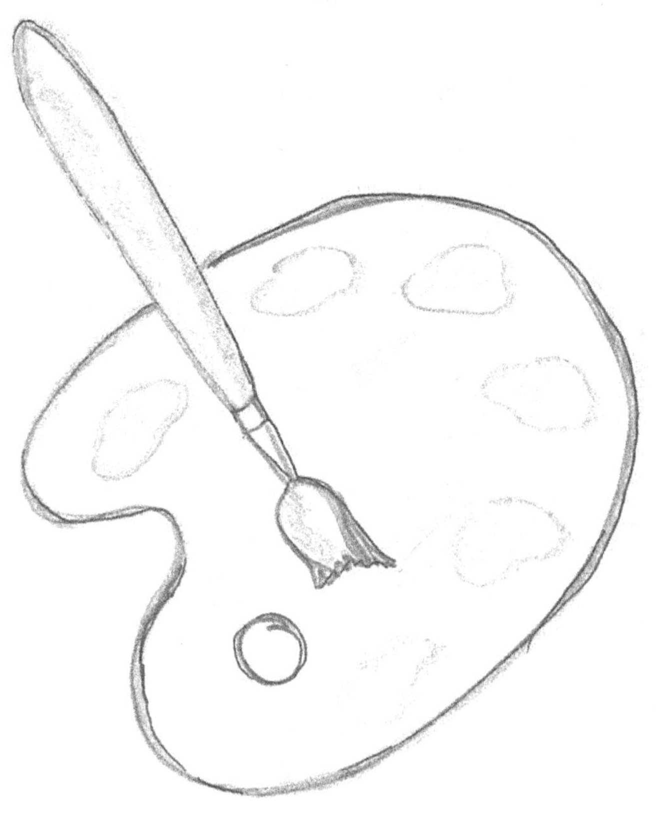

Creativity

Creativity can mean many things, like drawing or making paintings, but there is something about it that makes you unique and that many people would like to critique. It is something that people cannot take away, but the ideas it gives you may sweep you away. Nevertheless, no matter what it is, something big or something not big at all, it will always come from YOU!

Nighttime

The moon and the stars that shine in harmony; the dew on the leaves that fall so gently.

As the tiniest animal burrows into its nest, the baby owl tries to pass the hunting test.

The moon is finally full, and everything is still.

Goodnight to everyone. This day is done; now I will rest my head and wait until dawn.

Kindness

We speak of beauty as an outside thing when really it comes from within. The love we show should come from deep inside, deeper than our greatest likes on the outside. The more we try to spread this type of love around, means much more than you are bound to come around. So, then, no matter the problem, no matter the odds, no matter the people who try to bring you down, spread kindness all around.

And he said to him, "You shall love the Lord your God with all your heart and with all your soul and with all your mind. This is the great and first commandment. And the second is like it: You shall love your neighbor as yourself. On these two commandments depend all the Law and the Prophets."

— **Matthew 22: 37-40**

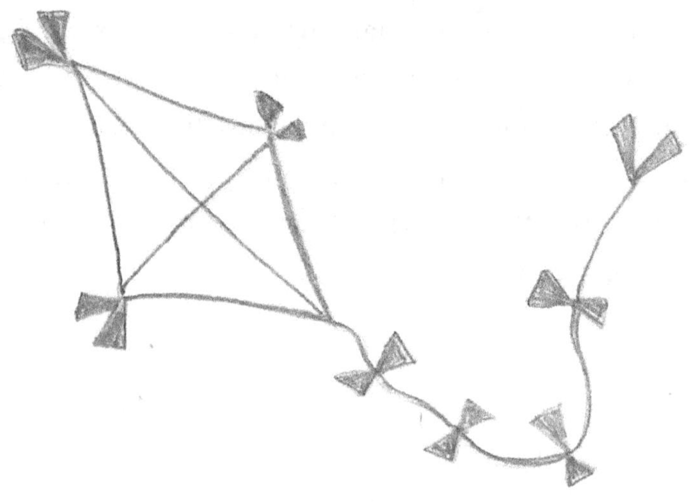

Colors

There are colors everywhere, such as in your food and your hair. A watermelon is red and green, and your hair may be blond or burgundy.

The sky has colors too, you know! Like the kites that soar and the big rainbow! Although, what are colors really? Are they just there, or do they have a meaning? The rainbow is a promise from God above to never bring such a big flood. Some colors mean certain things like royalty, and blue signifies both sky and sea. So, the colors portray many things for us to see.

Beautiful Butterfly

A beautiful butterfly with shades of black and white; when you see it, it is such a sight! You see the bright pigment of colors as its beautiful wings gently flutter. Slowly, it lands on a tulip's petal and peacefully rests, soon to settle.

Far Away

You pack your bags and get in the car; you drive for a little yet feel so far. You think to yourself, "Did I forget something?" Your mind says no, but something is nagging. You figure it out and turn around. You run inside, such a quiet sound. You get back in your car and continue to drive while thinking of your old home and life. You see the buildings, big and large, which soon disappear, replaced with huge forests, and you soon get drowned in fear. "My life was so different!" You say to yourself, "My little old bedroom and mom's wooden shelf." You finally make it to a five-hour drive that would have been four if not for that beehive. You take a step, then a few steps more. You finally make it, and then you knock on the door. You hear footsteps, and excitement takes over. Your fear goes away lower and lower.

The door opens, and someone steps out, "Please come in, ya little sprout!"

The Moonflower

A bud by day, a blossom at night. Beauty is so rare it's such a sight. Although just a figment of my imagination, I still call it a magnificent creation! The stars gather all around, not a peep nor a sound. It stands tall and fair as it sways with the air. The roots grow deep while you are counting sheep. It's a beauty no one can compare. Think of what we miss; it's such a despair. How do we know if we do not try? We only must leave one seeing eye. If a bud by day turns into a blossom at night, we just miss a beautiful sight. Beauty can be hidden, not necessarily forbidden. Dig a little deeper and turn every stone to discover the things that are unknown.

Age 13

Collectors

Collectors, often referred to as hoarders, collect tons of things but do have borders. For instance, maybe only plates from the 1980's or maybe anime collectors from the '20s. For one, I collected various book series and beanie babies from the 1990s.

Valley

One deep point, one deep dive. A shallow point: how will I survive?

A mountain top, a valley low, every day, everything is so slow.

How much more? Follow through, wait until tomorrow's dew.

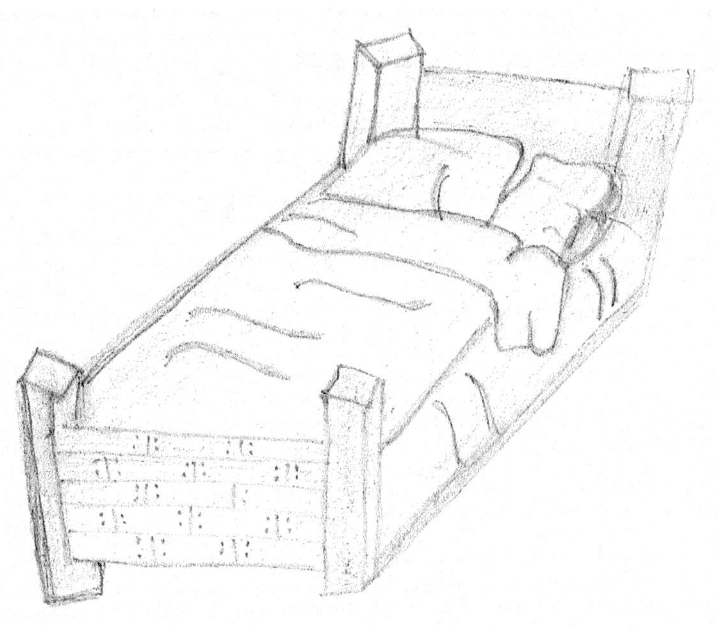

A Good Night's Rest

They say that fifteen minutes of laughing equals two hours of sleep. So, is a joke better than counting sheep? Compared to a comfy bed and a story read? Dreams you make inside your head. A good night's sleep may be hard to find, although it makes it easier for you to unwind. I will admit, a joke is good, but a good night's rest is more understood.

Age 14

A Little Lost

The walls and ceiling are gray; a small stick is all I must play with. Frigid wind chills me to the bone; where will this young child find a home? Vivid colors flood my view: warm yellows, reds, greens, and blue. People all gather around with joy, and laughter is the only sound. Millions of smells fill the air: candle flames and sweet-rich foods. The warmth of this place enchants me, and then the bite of cold wakes me to where I really am: reality.

The Sower

A world where all can see and hear, where there is beauty as well as fear.

But beauty is all but an appearance, masking an everlasting incoherence.

For many are blind to the truth, ignorant and have destined themselves to bear this evil fruit.

But there are some, some who strive, some who try and make things right.

"Listen! Behold, a sower went out to sow. And as he sowed, some seed fell along the path, and the birds came and devoured it. Other seed fell on rocky ground, where it did not have much soil, and immediately it sprang up, since it had no depth of soil. And when the sun rose, it was scorched, and since it had no root, it withered away. Other seeds fell among thorns, and the thorns grew up and choked it, and it yielded no grain. And other seeds fell into good soil and produced grain, growing up and increasing and yielding thirtyfold and sixtyfold and a hundredfold. And he said, "He who has ears to hear, let him hear."
-Mark 4:3-9

Dreading Time

A moment that begins in the blink of an eye, so many things have happened; man, how time flies! The excitement of the time thickens the air, but as of right now, I can only stare.

If the time really flew as fast as it felt, how long would it take for this moment to melt? I think of the day when I have to say goodbye, and all these feelings will also leave in the blink of an eye.

Life

Our lives are precious, and we keep them safe. Though we spare some, some are put to waste. How do we know that those children aren't smart? To have the ability to touch someone's heart. "The more, the merrier," some people say, yet all we do is kill and slay; therefore, I can say my own death was put at bay. I hope one day we all can smile and make every moment worthwhile.

> But Jesus said, "Let the little children come to me and do not hinder them, for such belongs in the kingdom of heaven."
>
> — Matthew 19:14

Writer's Block

What shall I do with this pen in my hand? Write out a story or twirl it around?

Think of my day... No, that's not the way. How can I flow my feelings onto this page?

How can I write when I have writer's block? My head is as hard as a rock.

You know what! I just found out; I was so annoyed I just read it aloud!

I hope you enjoyed it.

The World in Black and White

A statement that is simple and there are no hard parts. Like a picnic and a basket filled with freshly baked tarts. There is no need to stress to comprehend. There is no reason to do it in the end.

However, imagine the basket and its artful weave; the maker who made it worked hard to conceive.

On the other hand, the tarts inside, which were freshly baked flour, sugar, and cherries, would be great. Think of the setting in the world all around, where the birds chirp, and there is no sound. This simple statement may not always be quite right; the simple sentence, the world is in black and white.

These Old Walls

The walls in my room tell many stories, from baby pictures to paintings that hold many memories. These walls have watched me grow into who I am now, from silly phases and struggles, no doubt. These walls were seen when my brother put up my colorful ceiling fan and my mother read me a book about a girl in a faraway land. These walls saw when I first fell from my bed and when my father picked me up when I landed on my head. These walls were there when I put up all my posters and whenever my nephew helped me by climbing on my shoulders. These walls witnessed when I matured and when I got sick and was later cured. These walls recall when my mom tucked me in, way before my memories started to begin. And even now when I rise or fall, all the memories will be written on these old walls.

My Tiny Dog

My dog is a little bit more like a cat. She will sit on the couch or lie on your lap. She looks at you with menacing eyes; if there was any damage, she will tell you a lie. "The other dog did it, the one with gray fur. She jumped on the table and ate all your dinner." Then she will take over your bed, though she has one of her own, and take all your blankets, which she will not return. She looks at you with pleading eyes, eyes that say that she denies. "The other dog did it, the small one with black fur. He pooped on the carpet; I'm not your concern." She will take the treats she does not eat and hide them in corners out of greed. She will fight with the others if she disagrees. The other dogs try to make peace. She thinks she is the boss; she is in the dark, this little one, my tiny dog.

The Best Things Come Out of Disarray

What would happen if you feared tomorrow? Do you want to spend the rest of the day drowning in sorrow? The smallest things like what to eat or wear, these things we must prepare.

But if we were always worried, we'd have wasted today. I'd rather live in the moment than dread the next day. Don't get me wrong, preparing is great, but life happens, and things get in the way. So even the best plans, although well thought out and put together, can all fall apart in the stroke of a letter.

Spend time with loved ones and enjoy everything along the way because we don't know the time, the place, or the day it might all go away.

Don't be afraid when things don't go your way. Sometimes, the best things come out of disarray.

"Therefore do not be anxious about tomorrow,
for tomorrow will be anxious for itself.

Sufficient for the day is its own trouble."

— Matthew 6:34

Ten Years Old

A child extolled, adventurous, brave, and bold. Mind wide open, soaking up every experience, taking it all in. A sponge for knowledge, a curious mind, always something new to find. A heart of gold, full of love and appreciation kindness being his inspiration. A soul of innocence, untouched by the harsh realities of life, always seeing the best, even in strife.

Dedicated to Perseus Arion Olguin

Elfin

Deep in the forest, under a tree, where the promise of safety is not guaranteed. A miniature person, a legend, and a fairy tale survive in a life that is frail. During spring, when flowers bloom, the grass grows tall and blocks her door, just like a tomb. During summer, when the days are hot, her house is like an oven, and food begins to rot. In the fall, when the wind gets cool, she catches a break from her constant toil. But once winter comes with its howling storms, plants all die, and the leaves begin to mourn. So, you see, for creatures like me, the promise of safety is not guaranteed.

Selene A. Olguin

Vanity

In a world embellished with masks and misleading
displays lurks the existence of vanity forging the way.
A desire of appearance so grand,
shadows the truth with nasty lies in hand.

Like a dazzling gem, its beauty enchants,
enticing with stories of wealth that put you in a trance.
But vanity, my friend, is a temporary desire, a mirage
that expires.

For in the hollow pursuits, we find
an emptiness leaving too many hearts behind.
The obsession with oneself, the poison it generates,
blinds us from the natural beauty that truly resonates.

In the reflection of personality is where beauty is best
placed, not in the superficial, not in the long race.
For vanity fruits shallowness, devoid of strength,
leaving us grasping for substance, gasping for breath.

Let us uncover what we truly desire in our actions and
deeds, where kindness and compassion plant love-
filled seeds. Embrace humility, and let its wisdom
impart,
for it is genuine uprightness that sets ablaze the heart.

A life of purpose isn't measured by display,
but by the love and kindness we give away today. So,
cast aside the lure of vanity's snare,
and let our personalities be the clothing we wear.

School Days

Learning is a point of time with new beginnings;
paths filled up with challenges and various winnings.

In rooms filled with wisdom galore,
we explore many subjects we've never known before.
Math problems bewilder with numbers and grace,
while history unfolds its endless embrace.

Literature, a gateway to the mind and soul,
through tales and poems, we find experiences whole.
Science discloses nature's laws and wonders,
as we study space and all it has to discover.

Like a seed nourished deep in the ground,
learning new things is where growth can truly be
found.
Discovering passions, hobbies, and skills,
unraveling our potential with a burning will.

Coming to Age

With new friendships forged and bonds made strong,
we explore and travel the world, sometimes right,
sometimes painfully wrong. Through defeat and
success, we learn to survive and strive, embrace failures
and let our spirits thrive.

So, as you continue to embark on this uplifting quest,
remember, it's not just about being the best of the best.
It's about the lessons we learn and the constant joys
in this metamorphic journey, where growth employs.

In this period, a life-turning chapter unfolds,
a myriad of memories yet to unfold.
Accept the possibilities, take hold of the day,
for this year, a new chapter gets written onto a page.

A Smile Behind a Mask

In a world where masks are a normal attire and the experiences we have are bound to expire. A feeling could wash over like an ocean, but we could only see a tittynope of emotion. A deeper meaning can often be unseen. Dive deeper, because not everything is as it seems. A faint whisper of emotion or a conflict within, an eternal dilemma based on a whim. However, some of these feelings could be as pulchritudinous as a blooming flower and have an overwhelming ability to empower. But alas, this is also hidden, even if we stay to listen. So let the truth be told: understanding a person is no easy task; some choose to smile under a mask.

15 Years Old

The Path

There will be days when the sun shines its brightest. Bathes flowers in light and paints the meadows in vibrant greens. And somewhere the light slowly drips and leaves the sky at its darkest. Gives an eerie pale glow, and paints black and white scenes. But there is always a path that connects the two. Sometimes one side is easier to cross than the other. And right now, you may have a dreadful view. Inevitably you will end up seeing another.

Nothing Lasts Forever

Please, tell me why.
We miss the moments right before our eyes and why
people come and go so fast.

And why, is it that nothing said, yet you hear it all so
clearly.
And why, is it that
everything seem to crumble all too quickly.

Please tell me why, only after a story ends we feel it and
why, oh why does change hurt so much one can hardly
bear it.

Apparently, nothing lasts forever.

Memories

The books that you've read and the memories you've been told. The pages they bent, crinkle, and fold. The stories you have shared and the struggles you have faced, eventually will be forgotten at some point or place. Things you have collected, kept close, and held dear will be given away, sold, or forgotten, I fear. The time will come, when we are no longer here. When the world goes on without us being anywhere near. But, what's hardest to bear is the feeling one holds when they find out they will miss out on far more than they know.

My Room

Warm lighting emits a golden glow
and windows are drawn closed.
A quilted blanket on the bed:
the past owner, now a ghost.
Book-lined shelves fill empty spaces,
adding color as well as feel.
Each holding worlds of their own
with characters that feel all too real.
Knick knacks made of wool and clay
all made by hand.
Not there for any actual reason
other than to calm my mind's strange land.
Clothing often littering the floor
after moments of tribulation.
Hangers equally mocking my weekly cleanings
momentarily ending my aspirations.
Although life can be uncomfortable and disappointing,
and, sometimes, we get overcome by the gloom.
I personally have a way to unwind:
spending some time alone in my room.

Beautiful Creatures

Can someone tell me why these things caught my
heart,
why I consider them God's work of art.
Most people think of them to be revolting.
But, believe it or not, some have beauty worth
beholding.
Some are exploding with colors and some are just plain
cute.
Some are shiny and pretty and some look like they are
always in a bad mood.
You may find them sticky and yucky but I find them
adorable.
So, if you still think frogs are gross, hopefully, after
reading this poem, it's reversible.

Why?

Why can't my ideas flow endlessly onto a page?
Preferably in correct grammar and decent vocabulary?
Why is it so hard to put my thoughts into words?
Honestly, it's annoying and quite unnecessary.
Why can't my writing flow as other author's writings
do?
Is it too much to ask that my pen be my friend?
That my facts stay true and that my plots don't
descend?
Lately, I've been trying not to hit this common wall,
but writers' block eventually and unfortunately comes
to visit us all.

Ba'dink!

From a Simple Text

Beginning all from a simple text.
Unimportant, but remember when I had to vent and gave you a front row seat?
That's when it started. A night long conversation.
Turning an acquaintance into a friend never missing a beat.
Checking message after message, no moment was dull.
However often a topic arose, even that was substantial.
Even through the screens of our laptop or phone, we managed to build up and grow a friendship in both our time zones.
Eventually I hope we could meet up one day cause the ride by car would be a long way.
Knowing everything about me despite the space apart.
And in every text, call, and song you'll always be in my heart.
Lastly, I would like to say thank you so much.
You mean a great deal to me, and I pray we never lose touch.

About the Author

Selene Olguin was born in Harlingen Texas, 2009 and is the daughter of Angel and Rose Olguin, who are both science teachers. Starting from blue sticky notes and mini notebooks, she eventually wrote her first book at ten years old **'Animal Tails'** after one abstruse math quiz and to her surprise got it published at age eleven. From there she began giving motivational speeches to schools encouraging other children--even though she too was still starting out- and even got to meet a few others that encouraged her. She then went on to submit a few of her poems to the La Feria and Los Fresnos Texas newspaper and with the help of the owner and editor got a job as a journalist. She joined the Valley Byliners (a non-profit organization of authors) and has now published 'A Poetic Journey.'

'A Poetic Journey' is a collection of Selene's poems starting from the age eleven up to the age of fifteen showing her growth in writing through the years.

Special Thanks

Special thanks to my brother Angel Olguin V and my sister-in-law Dinora Olguin, who helped me edit my poems. Thank you so much for all my family's guidance and support.